BRITISH ATLANTEANS

MIKE RHODES

AMBERLEY

First published 2025

Amberley Publishing
The Hill, Stroud
Gloucestershire, GL5 4EP

www.amberley-books.com

Copyright © Mike Rhodes, 2025

The right of Mike Rhodes to be identified as
the Author of this work has been asserted in
accordance with the Copyrights, Designs and
Patents Act 1988.

ISBN 978 1 3981 2325 0 (print)
ISBN 978 1 3981 2326 7 (ebook)

British Library Cataloguing in Publication Data.
A catalogue record for this book is available from
the British Library.

Origination by Amberley Publishing.
Printed in the UK.

Appointed GPSR EU Representative: Easy Access
System Europe Oü, 16879218
Address: Mustamäe tee 50, 10621, Tallinn, Estonia
Contact Details: gpsr.requests@easproject.com,
+358 40 500 3575

Introduction

The Leyland Atlantean is a British phenomenon. Its development, manufacture and use in service spanned more than half a century. Today it can still be seen on the roads of Britain either in the form of a preserved vehicle or as an open-top bus. Its development began in the early 1950s when work was carried out at Leyland Motors to produce a rear-engined double-deck bus. Two prototypes were initially produced, one in 1954 and a second the year after. These carried the registrations STF 90 and XTC 684 (pictured below) respectively, and bore little resemblance to what would emerge as the finished article. They were powered by a 0.350 engine and were known as the 'Lowloader'. It would be another three years before the first fully developed model was road tested.

The *Commercial Motor Magazine* of 17 October 1958 ran a story describing what was claimed to be the first road test of the new Atlantean. The pictures accompanying the article depicted the bus, which had been fitted with an Alexander-built H44/34F body, running in the centre of nearby (to Leyland) Preston. Classified as a PDR1, it subsequently passed to Glasgow Corporation, initially as a demonstrator and then as a permanent acquisition. It was Glasgow's sole example for approaching nearly three years before it was initially chosen as the replacement

for the undertaking's trolleybuses, which were gradually being phased out between 1962 and 1967. From October 1962 through to May 1981 Glasgow took delivery of a further 1,448 Atlanteans and accumulated the largest and most standardised fleet of the type anywhere in the world. All were bodied by Walter Alexander's of Falkirk.

The first operator to place the type into daily service was James of Ammanford, closely followed by Wallasey Corporation in mid-December 1958. Wallasey would go on to operate thirty of the type, all of which were bodied by Metro-Cammell. Despite the first Atlantean being bodied by Alexander, Leyland had obviously worked closely with Metro-Cammell Weymann as all the Atlanteans produced up until December 1959 were finished with bodywork assembled by either Metro-Cammell's Washwood Heath plant or at the Weymann factory in Addlestone. Alexander re-entered the fray in January 1960 with batches of buses for three operators in the North East. The monopoly was finally broken in March 1960 when Roe completed a batch of twenty-three Atlanteans for Trent Motor Services.

In the early years both Metro-Cammell and Weymann produced lowbridge models for a number of operators. These included East Midland, James of Ammanford, J. Fishwick & Sons, Maidstone & District, Potteries Motor Traction, Ribble Motor Services, Trent Motor Services and Yorkshire Traction. A solitary lowbridge bus was also built for Walsall Corporation, whilst the last of any lowbridge models were the three supplied to J. Fishwick & Sons in June 1966. A fourth body builder did not enter the arena until April 1963 when East Lancashire Coachbuilders completed eight Atlanteans for Bolton Corporation. Over a twenty-six-year production period (1958–84) eighteen different body builders supplied 105 different operators with completed buses. A breakdown of the numbers is shown below. The figures are open to scrutiny and have not been compiled from official records but have been produced from a combination of various sources.

Walter Alexander & Sons (Coachbuilders) Ltd, Falkirk (1947)	3,999
Metro-Cammell Carriage & Wagon Co. (MCCW/MCW), Birmingham (1932)	1,524
Charles H. Roe Ltd, Crossgates, Leeds (1917)	1,483
Northern Counties Motor & Engineering Co., Wigan (1919)	1,312
Park Royal Vehicles, Brent, London (1889)	1,277
East Lancashire Coachbuilders Ltd, Blackburn (1934)	1,101
Weymann Motor Bodies Ltd, Addlestone (1925)	494
Eastern Coach Works Ltd, Lowestoft (1920)	253
Willowbrook Coachbuilders Ltd, Loughborough (1927)	119*
W. Alexander & Co. (Belfast) Ltd, Mallusk, County Antrim (1969)	80
Neepsend Coachworks Ltd, Pennine Road, Sheffield (1963)	49
Marshall Coachbuilders Ltd, Cambridge (1946)	33
Massey Brothers Ltd, Pemberton (1904)	31
Pennine Coachcraft (Seddon Motors Ltd), Royton, Oldham (1937)	12
M. H. Coachworks Ltd, Belfast (William Potter, Belfast) (1960)	3
W. H. Fowler, Leyland (1968)	1
Neoplan, Stuttgart, Germany (1935)	1
Van Hool McArdle, Spa Road, Dublin (1972)	1
	11,773

* Includes six completed by Northern Counties.
Date company founded or established in brackets.

As can be seen Alexander's provided the greatest number of completed buses by some margin. The initial design was somewhat of a flat-fronted model before the company's trademark rounded-front design was introduced on Glasgow's first production models in October 1962. By the end of the 1960s Alexander had introduced the attractive and timeless peaked-dome model, which first appeared on Merseyside PTE's first batch of 'Jumbos' and was also greatly favoured by a number of operators. A more rounded panoramic-window version also became available from late 1972.

Whilst Alexander's topped the production numbers, at the opposite end of the scale were Fowler, Neoplan and Van Hool with just a single bus apiece. The latter built the bodywork on a large batch of Volvo Ailsas for South Yorkshire PTE and also completed the bodywork on just one Atlantean which was tagged on to the end of the order. Meanwhile Fowler only ever built eleven bus bodies, which comprised one minibus, nine single-deck saloons and a solitary double-decker on an Atlantean chassis – the latter was not that pleasing on the eye.

Operators tended to stay loyal to their local body builder. As already mentioned, Glasgow's entire complement of Atlanteans was bodied by the Scottish firm, as was Edinburgh/Lothian's 588 Atlanteans. Aberdeen/Grampian's entire fleet of 199 Atlanteans was also completed with Alexander-built bodies. Meanwhile, after using four different body builders for their first four batches of Atlanteans, Leeds City Transport/West Yorkshire PTE then stayed loyal to Roe, eventually taking a further 571 of the type with locally built bodywork. Similarly, Kingston-upon-Hull's entire fleet of 241 Atlanteans, except the first five, were also bodied by Roe.

Greater Manchester struck up a partnership with nearby Northern Counties, who produced what was referred to as the Manchester Standard with the same style of body being adopted for Atlanteans, Daimler Fleetlines and Leyland Fleetlines. Virtually all the Lancashire municipal operators had their fair share of East Lancs-bodied Atlanteans. Only Burnley Colne & Nelson did not operate any Atlanteans, preferring to run Bristol VRTs, by which time the operator had become known as Burnley & Pendle.

Some fleets standardised on one or two body builders; for example Southampton City Transport operated a fleet of 175 virtually identical East Lancs-bodied Atlanteans, all of which had the same seating configuration. In the other extreme Sheffield City Transport and its successors operated a fleet of buses with nine different body styles. Besides the solitary Van Hool example, Sheffield also bought three batches of buses, amounting to forty vehicles in total, with bodies constructed locally by Neepsend Coachbuilders together with the only batch of double-deck Marshall-bodied Atlanteans, which consisted of thirty buses. The only other operators to receive buses bodied by Neepsend were Bolton and Oldham whilst the only other Atlanteans bodied by Marshall were three single-deckers for Great Yarmouth Corporation.

Indeed the Atlantean PDR1 chassis was capable of receiving single-deck bodywork but only two other operators availed themselves of this option. Portsmouth City Transport took delivery of twelve Seddon-bodied B40D PDR2/1s in June 1971 whilst Merseyside PTE received two Northern Counties-bodied similar chassis types (originally ordered by Birkenhead Corporation), also of a B40D configuration, in January 1971. The only other single-deck Atlanteans that ever existed were not entirely new buses. Fylde Transport (Blue Buses) had four of their ex-Hull Atlanteans rebodied by Northern Counties as single-deck buses in 1993, which were known as Paladins. They later passed to Blackpool Transport with the Fylde undertaking.

Atlanteans were purchased by a variety of operators throughout the UK including Belfast Corporation/Citybus and Ulsterbus in Northern Ireland. One area, however, which was somewhat bereft of the type was the Midlands as this was the stronghold of the Daimler Fleetline, the Atlantean's principal competitor. Besides Walsall's solitary bus, Birmingham City Transport had just eleven examples (including an ex-demonstrator) and Coventry City Transport, somewhat controversially, added twenty-two of the type with Willowbrook bodywork to their fleet in 1965.

The Atlantean was a functional bus built mainly for stage carriage work, although a small number of operators did specify a more upmarket interior. The first to do so was Ribble/Standerwick who presented Weymann with an exacting specification which was applied to thirty-seven buses. These had only sixteen seats on the lower deck and were fitted out with a cold-food serving galley and a toilet and were intended for use on long-distance motorway services between Lancashire/Cumberland and London. Silver Star of Porton in Wiltshire received a single coach-seated example in June 1961 whilst the airline BOAC specified coach-style seats in their buses for the Victoria to Heathrow Airport transfer service. Alexander built a batch of twenty coach-seated Atlanteans for the Tyne & Wear PTE in December 1980 whilst Blackpool Transport, Fylde, City of Lancaster and Borough of Preston all specified enhanced seating in at least two of their new intake of buses in the early 1980s.

Possibly the strangest order received by Leyland Motors was that from Hale Trent Cakes of Clevedon (Somerset). Registered HHT 57N, the bus was bodied by East Lancashire Coachbuilders to their standard design except that it had no destination screen. It was not classed as a PSV and was used by Hale Trent, along with a number of other buses, as staff transport. Equally odd was the completion of a vehicle by Neoplan for a religious society, which became the last 'new' Atlantean to be registered in 1988.

The Atlantean chassis designation was initially PDR1/1 (Passenger Double-deck Rear-engine), which was powered by a 0.600 or 0.680 engine. There were also a number of variants that were produced until 1972. Initially the chassis was designed to accommodate a 30-foot-long (later increased to 30 feet 10 inches) body but from 1966 a 33-foot-long option also became available. In 1972, following a prolonged period of research and development, the model was relaunched as the AN68 where the '68' referred to the engine capacity. Again as the years progressed there were several variants including a left-hand-drive option and an AN69 (0.690 engine) model.

Production of the Atlantean chassis for the home market ceased in October 1984 with Fylde Borough Transport's No. 75 taking the honours. By this time the Atlantean's successor, the Olympian, had become firmly established. However, the chassis continued to be built for a further two years for the overseas market. The first Atlanteans sold abroad had gone to South Africa in 1960 and not unsurprisingly they had Metro-Cammell bodies. Other prominent overseas customers included Baghdad, Dublin (CIE), Kuwait, Oporto, Singapore, Stockholm, Sydney (DGT) and Tehran. The Stockholm order was for fifty buses which had 36-foot-long bodies constructed by Park Royal Vehicles and were the only Atlanteans over 33 feet long to be built for either the home or overseas market. Around a further 3,529 Atlanteans went abroad making a grand total of 15,301, give or take the odd one or two.

If nothing else, the Atlantean was certainly an enduring bus. The photographs are arranged in alphabetical order of body constructor and then in manufacture date order within each group. With such an extensive subject to cover it is impossible to illustrate every variation of Atlantean, but I am confident a representative balance has been achieved across the various body styles and operators. I am indebted to a number of contributors for permission to use their photographs, which have been accredited accordingly.

Atlantean Chassis Types

Model	Engine	Gearbox	Brakes	Wheel Base	Body Length	Width	Years in Build
PDR1/1	600	Pneum.	Air	195in.	360in.	96in.	1958–67
PDR1A/1	680	Pneum.	Air	195in.	360in.	96in.	1967–72
PDR1/2#	600	Pneum.	Air	195in.	360in.	96in.	1964–67
PDR1/3	600	Pneum.	Air	195in.	360in.	96in.	1967–71
PDR2/1	680	Pneum.	Air	222in	390in.	96in.	1966–72
AN68/1R	680	Pneum.	Air	195in.	370in.	96in.	1972–76
AN68/2R	680	Pneum.	Air	222in.	393in.	96in.	1972–76
AN68A/1R*	680	Pneum.	Air	195in.	370in.	96in.	1975–84
AN68A/2R*	680	Pneum.	Air	222in.	393in.	96in.	1975–84
AN68B/1R	680	Pneum.	Air	195in.	370in.	96in.	1979–80
AN68B/2R	680	Pneum.	Air	222in.	393in.	96in	1979–80
AN68C/1R	680	Pneum.	Air	195in.	370in.	96in.	1980–82
AN68C/2R	680	Pneum.	Air	222in.	393in.	96in	1980–82
AN68D/1R	680	Pneum.	Air	195in.	370in.	96in.	1982–84
AN68D/2R	680	Pneum.	Air	222in.	393in.	96in	1982–84

Left-hand drive models had the suffix 'L'.
Daimler gearbox; * G2 gearbox.

Sources

Bus Lists on the Web (https://www.buslistsontheweb.co.uk/)
Jack, Doug, *The Leyland Bus Mk2* (Glossop: Transport Publishing Co., 1984)
Local Transport History Library

Alexander

What became Glasgow's first Atlantean is widely regarded as being the first to be thoroughly road tested by Leyland Motors in late 1958. This followed several years of development and a number of prototypes. The seventy-eight-seat body was constructed by Walter Alexander and it was the Corporation's only Atlantean for nearly three years. Having been withdrawn in 1973, No. LA1 eventually passed to the Glasgow Vehicle Trust Museum at Bridgeton. (Iain Lawson)

Another one-off was Belfast Corporation (later Citybus) PDR1/1 No. 551, which is seen in Donegal Square South in the late 1960s. This bus was new in April 1960. It later passed to Lough Swilly with whom it carried the number 143. It was scrapped in 2002. (slimy)

Glasgow Corporation started to replace its trolleybuses in late 1962 and had decided on the Alexander-bodied Atlantean following prolonged consultations with the body builder. Number LA124 was one of the initial batch of 160. Having been repainted in to the Greater Glasgow PTE livery, it remained in service until late 1975 when it was sold to Paul Sykes dealership at Barnsley, where it is seen on 27 February 1976.

Newcastle Corporation bought its first forty Alexander-bodied Atlanteans in February 1960. The operator and its successors continued to favour the type until 1980, predominantly with Alexander bodywork. The early ones had the flat front style of body as depicted here on 1963 PDR1/1 Atlantean No. 119 (originally Newcastle No. 19), which was photographed in Grainger Street in the city centre on 26 May 1976. The Trustee Savings Bank is now a Wetherspoons named the 'Mile Castle' and the building dates from 1810.

Edinburgh Corporation received its first Atlantean in February 1966 followed by a production batch of twenty-five in October. These were of the Glasgow style but had panoramic windows. Pioneer No. 801 is preserved and is seen in Northfield Broadway in Edinburgh on 13 April 2019 on a vintage bus running day. The local authority went on to operate 588 Atlanteans, all with Alexander bodies.

Ribble Motors of Preston bought a batch of ten PDR1/2s with Alexander 'H' designated bodies in 1966, the only such labelled vehicles other than Western SMT No. 2137. Number 1867 was photographed in Lightfoot Lane in Preston on 29 November 1977 on the jointly operated (with Preston Borough) P2 service to Penwortham.

Newcastle bought a batch of twenty-eight similar-looking buses in August 1966, although these had six more seats than the Ribble Atlanteans. Originally Newcastle No. 257 but now carrying the PTE logo and the number 457, this example is seen outside St Hilda's parish church in South Shields on 26 May 1976.

KUS 599E had been new to Glasgow Corporation in May 1967 as No. LA344. Now wearing the colours of OK Motors of Bishop Auckland, it was photographed at the garage on 26 June 1982. Keeping it company are former Colchester Corporation Massey/PD2A OVX 143D and Emmerson Roe/PD3/6 YUP 487.

Newport Corporation was another municipal operator that favoured Alexander bodywork on its Atlantean chassis. From 1966–71 the authority bought six batches of Atlanteans, totalling forty-three buses, all with Alexander 'A' type bodies. Number 77 was new in 1968 and is seen in Newport bus station on 14 April 1976.

Bournemouth Corporation bought its first Atlanteans in 1964 but the first two batches were bodied by Weymann and Metro-Cammell. They also had batches of similar-looking Daimler Fleetlines. Number 230 was new in April 1969 and survived into preservation. It is seen in the centre of Lytham St Annes taking part in a vintage running day on 26 August 2019.

In December 1969 Alexander produced the first buses with the 'peaked dome' style for Merseyside PTE. Numbers 1111–50 were of a chassis type designated PDR2/1. They acquired the name of 'Jumbos' due to their 33-foot length and were fitted with seventy-nine seats in a dual-door body configuration. Although they were the first new buses for the PTE, they initially wore the Corporation green. Class leader No. 1111 survived into preservation and is part of the Merseyside Transport Trust collection based at Burscough, where it was photographed on 9 July 2017. Later repainted into PTE colours, No. 1111 was photographed at Southport Pleasureland on 15 August 1976. Two further batches of the type were purchased in 1971, bringing the total operated up to 125.

In 1982 Isle of Man National Transport acquired ten of Merseyside's Jumbos. IOMNT No. 43 had been MPTE No. 1142. It passed to Citibus of Chadderton in November 1988 and was scrapped three years later. It is seen at Derby Castle on the Isle of Man on 28 May 1983.

The A1-Bus Owners Association collectively had a mixed bag of both second-hand and new buses. PAG 759H was a PDR1A/1 owned by T. Hunter of Kilmarnock. It is seen in Boglemart Street in Stevenston on 27 March 1976. A total of twenty-six new Atlanteans were operated by the Association. The corner building was a dental surgery in 2023.

In total Edinburgh Corporation/Lothian Buses bought nineteen batches of Atlanteans from 1966–81. Number 390 was one of fifty buses that were new in 1970. Apart from the first seventy-five and last six Atlanteans, the vast majority were the two-door version. This is a typical scene of the era in Princes Street recorded on 18 April 1981.

Bournemouth's (Yellow Buses) penultimate batch of Atlanteans were Nos 250–65 purchased in December 1970. All of the operator's Atlanteans were single-door. Number 258 was photographed in the garage yard at Mallard Road on 15 March 1975. Opened in 1951, it was closed as a bus garage in 2007. The building is now listed and houses a B&M store. Yellow Buses ceased trading in August 2022.

Bradford Corporation also had some Atlanteans similar in appearance to MPTE's Jumbos but the first twenty, which were new in July 1971, were only 30 feet long. Number 449 (WYPTE No. 2449) is seen in Bradford Town Hall Square on 8 November 1975. Behind is one of Bradford's prolific Regent Vs. This area has since been pedestrianised.

Isle of Man National Transport also bought sixteen redundant Atlanteans from the Tyneside PTE. Number 64 was new to the PTE in 1972 as No. 677. It was withdrawn in June 1986. After passing to several owners it was eventually scrapped in 2001. It is seen in New Road at Laxey on 28 May 1983 working on service 15 from Douglas to Ramsey.

Cunninghams Bus Service Ltd was a local operator based in Paisley that bought seven new Atlanteans over a ten-year period from 1967. LXS 14K was a PDR1A/1 model which joined the fleet in May 1972. It is seen in the garage yard at Underwood Road on 23 April 1976. The operator was acquired by Western SMT on 12 August 1979.

Leyland Motors had been working on an improved version of the Atlantean for a considerable time and finally introduced the new designated AN68/1R or 2R to the market in May 1972. The first with Alexander bodies were delivered to the Merseyside PTE in September. Numbering 100, they introduced the classic 'AL' peak-domed style. Numbers 1340 and 1535 (new in December 1972/3, respectively) are seen in St John's Lane in Liverpool city centre on 9 April 1983.

Edinburgh seemed to favour the panoramic window style of body, as demonstrated on these two examples. Number 17 was an AN68/1R of 1972 whilst No. 484 was an AN68A/1R, which was new in 1976. Both were fitted with the improved 0.680 engine. They are seen in St Andrew Square in the city centre on 10 August 1983. Lothian's last Atlantean bowed out of service on 3 January 2000.

Sheffield/South Yorkshire PTE was an enthusiastic exponent of the Atlantean and bought no fewer than 653 of the type over a twenty-two-year period. Amongst the nine different body builders called upon were a number with Alexander bodies. Number 295 was new to Sheffield Transport in March 1973 and is seen in Pond Street bus station on 22 May 1976.

Southport Corporation ordered ten Atlanteans in 1972; these were dual-door buses that entered service in May/June 1973. Number 89 was photographed in Lord Street on 27 May 1975, by which time it had become No. 0089 in the Merseyside PTE fleet. Note the different lower-front arrangement from the Sheffield vehicle.

Around the same time Portsmouth City Transport received its second batch of Alexander-bodied Atlanteans. Number 273 is seen in The Hard on 12 June 1976. Portsmouth would go on to operate ninety dual-door Alexander-bodied Atlanteans. The King & Queen and Ship Anson public houses had both been rebuilt in 1922.

Aberdeen/Grampian amassed a fleet of 199 Alexander-bodied Atlanteans from 1967–83. They also favoured dual-door bodywork. Apart from the first ten they were all of the improved AN68 version. Number 164 was one of an order for twenty-four of the type which was received in 1973. It is pictured in Castle Street on 26 March 1983 alongside the Mercat Cross, which was designed by John Montgomery and dates from 1686.

Grampian No. 160 was of the same batch but was one of around a dozen former Grampian (Aberdeen) Atlanteans acquired by City of Lancaster after deregulation. It is seen at the former Morecambe & Heysham Corporation garage, with another of the type behind, on 29 March 1992.

Procters of Hanley in Staffordshire operated just two new Atlanteans. GBF 278/9N were a pair of AN68/1Rs with Alexander H45/31F bodies purchased in October 1974. The second of the duo is pictured at Blackpool on 19 June 1977 having brought a party of day-trippers to the seaside. It would have been more at home plying its trade between Leek and Cheddleton. Procter went out of business in 2013. Blackpool Transport's Rigby Road bus garage is in the background.

Borough of Preston didn't buy any Atlanteans until 1974, having bought 'OMO' single-deck types in the preceding six years. First of the new order, No. 101, is seen with the first Panther, No. 201, on 'Baths Special' duty in Lancaster Road on 17 November 1977. All but the last two of Preston's Atlanteans were originally 33-foot-long dual-door models.

Number 110 was the last of Preston's initial batch of ten new in 1974/5. In 1991 Nos 101/8–10 were sold to Hyndburn Transport after having the centre doors removed. Seen sporting a modified front end, Hyndburn No. 210 (ex-PBT Bo. 110) is pictured passing Accrington Town Hall in Blackburn Road on 16 March 1991. It was scrapped in 2009.

A busy scene at The Hard in Portsmouth on 22 April 1978. Alexander-bodied Atlanteans Nos 297 and 318 are seen with Metro-Cammell-bodied example No. 247. The Alexanders are from two separate batches obtained in 1975 and are mounted on AN68/1R-type chassis. The authority purchased fifteen more in 1978, followed by another ten the year after. The last ten Atlanteans had East Lancs bodies.

Another former Glasgow Atlantean is seen in the colours of Rossendale Transport on 24 August 1985. This is former Greater Glasgow PTE No. LA981, which was new in 1975 and became surplus to requirements before its time. It has paused in Rawtenstall bus station whilst working a service 4 duty from Bacup to Accrington.

Two more Atlanteans owned by members of the A1 consortium are seen at J. C. Stewart's garage in Boglemart Street in Stevenston on 12 April 1978; both buses were new in July 1976. They are NCS 13P belonging to Dunn and NCS 14P, which was on home territory. The garage site is now occupied by a Lidl convenience store and a petrol station.

Two for the price of one as Northern (originally Gateshead & District) No. 129 passes Tyne & Wear PTE No. 312 outside Newcastle Civic Centre on the Great North Road on 4 April 1979. The Northern bus was new in May 1965 and has an earlier style of bodywork compared to the PTE bus, which dates from 1978.

The Glasgow PTE was still buying new Alexander-bodied Atlanteans in 1979 and indeed continued to do so until 1981 when the last of an eventual 1,449 of the type was put in to service. No. LA1254, now labelled as 'Trans-Clyde', was photographed in Jamaica Street on 29 May 1984.

After purchasing three batches of East Lancs-bodied Atlanteans, Borough of Preston reverted to Alexander for the next ten. Numbers 143/5/4 are pictured at the bus station on 22 April 1980 only a few weeks after entering service. The destination screens were lower down than those on Nos 101–10.

All ten of the batch were sold on to other operators with Nos 144/7–50 passing to J. Fishwick & Sons of nearby Leyland in October 2000. Another minor accident victim, No. 148 (Fishwick No. 24), is back on home territory in Garstang Road in Preston on 25 September 2002 working a school special. Number 148 was scrapped in 2007.

Greater Glasgow changed its identity again in 1980, to Strathclyde PTE. Finally shedding the green and yellow, No. LA1394, new in October 1980, is seen in West Regent Street on 27 July 1989. The last Atlanteans operating for the PTE were taken out of service in November 1998, with No. LA1408 being the last one in use.

A revisit to Rawtenstall on 10 June 1994 found former South Yorkshire PTE Alexander-bodied example No. 190 (ex-SYPTE and new in 1981 as No. 1790) parked up at the bus station in Bacup Road. Along with thirty Marshall-bodied Atlanteans, these had been the last of the type to join the PTE with eight of the batch passing to Rossendale in 1991. They had originally been dual-door buses.

The last of Lothian Buses' 588 Atlanteans were six received in November 1981, which were for the Airport service. These were the first single-door type since 1968 and, as can be seen, they were specially painted white and black. Number 664 is seen on Waverley Bridge on 10 August 1983.

Grampian (Scottish), formerly Aberdeen Corporation, was another operator that remained loyal to the Alexander-bodied Atlantean. Two of the last to join the fleet were Nos 332 and 341, which are seen when virtually brand new on 26 March 1983 in the garage yard at King Street. This is now the location of the FirstBus Group Administrative Building.

Merseyside PTE No. 1070 had several claims to fame. It was the last Atlantean received by the PTE in May 1984 and the last of the type (3,999th) to be bodied by Alexander. It was also the penultimate Atlantean to enter service in the UK. Saved for preservation following withdrawal in 2001 and now painted in Mersey Travel livery (MTL), it is seen at Birkenhead Woodside on 2 October 2016. The replica Hong Kong trams from the Wirral Transport Museum can be seen behind.

Alexander Belfast

Alexander's also had a subsidiary works in Belfast, which was responsible for completing buses for both Northern Ireland and the Republic operators. Ulsterbus received a batch of forty PDR2/1s with Alexander Belfast bodies in 1971. Number 911 was photographed in Portrush in September 1979 heading for nearby Colraine on service 140. Although Ulsterbus didn't purchase anymore new Atlanteans, they did acquire some second-hand examples in the late 1980s from Edinburgh and Glasgow. (Michael Cleary)

Following their experience with No. 551 in the early 1960s, Belfast Citybus purchased three more in 1964 with M. H. Coachworks bodies and then a batch of forty with Alexander bodies in 1975. Number 2891 is seen in Donegal Square North sometime in 1982 working to Mount Merrion via the Shankill Road. Citybus also had quite a number of similarly bodied Fleetlines. Behind is the former Water Office, which dates from 1860–79. (John Law)

East Lancs

After buying a mixture of front-engined types of double-deck buses, Bolton Transport obtained their first Atlanteans in April 1963. These were a batch of eight and were the first Atlanteans to be bodied by the Blackburn-based concern. Greater Manchester Transport's No. 6710 (originally Bolton Transport No. 210) was one of the second batch from East Lancs, which was obtained in April 1964. It was photographed close to Bridgeman Street garage on 30 October 1975.

Many of the Lancashire municipal fleets turned to East Lancs to construct the bodywork on Atlantean chassis. Oldham Corporation generally favoured Roe bodywork but their second batch of Atlanteans were bodied by East Lancs (ELC) in 1966. Here GMT No. 5134 (originally Oldham Corporation No. 134) was found nestling inside the former authority's bus garage in Oldham on 3 August 1975. The peaked dome and curved windscreen became standard features of the early ELC models.

Blackburn Corporation didn't really have any choice when it came to bodywork for their buses in general. The development of the ELC styles can be followed throughout the fleet from 1968–84. Number 52 was one of the first batch of ten and is pictured in the Boulevard on 18 June 1977 in commemorative 'Silver Jubilee' livery.

Southampton City Transport also amassed a large fleet of 175 East Lancs-bodied Atlanteans from 1968–81, all of which were of the same style and seating configuration. Number 115 was new in 1968 and is seen in Above Bar Street in the city centre on 12 June 1976. Southampton's last Atlanteans were withdrawn in 2005.

Accrington Corporation/Hyndburn Transport bought their buses in small numbers with the Atlantean being the preferred double-decker from 1969–80. Number 172 was one of three purchased in 1969 whilst No. 188 was one of four dating from 1976, by which time a flat windscreen had become an option. They are seen in the garage yard on 22 April 1982.

The last batch of Atlanteans ordered by Bolton Transport weren't delivered until January 1972 and were received in SELNEC colours. These were some of the last PDR2/1 (32-foot 9-inch) chassis types to be built. No. 6814 is seen in Haymarket Street in Bury on 23 October 1982 on the long-standing service (5)23, which plied between Bolton and Bury for many years.

Not all of East Lancs' regular customers were operators in Lancashire as both Eastbourne and Brighton Corporations were loyal recipients. The former bought a total of twenty-seven ELC-bodied Atlanteans in six batches from 1972–80. Number 14 of the first batch is seen in the Churchdale Road garage yard on 3 June 1975. Number 18 of 1975 is alongside.

City of Lancaster No. 87, along with Nos 84/5/9, led an interesting life. It was new in 1972 to Blackburn Corporation. The quartet (plus one for spares) was snapped up by Lancaster in 1985 with three of the group having been converted to open-top buses. It is seen at Heysham Village on 26 August 1985. They survived until the takeover by Stagecoach in 1993.

Caerphilly bought three Atlanteans in October 1973. These were joined by two more for the renamed Rhymney Valley DC fleet in April 1975. Number 40, one of the original trio, is seen outside Caerphilly railway station on 2 July 1977 with a group of RVDC buses. Caerphilly buses had previously been painted blue and white.

It could be difficult to distinguish the bodywork on Nottingham's (NCT) buses as the operator specified a similar style from their principal suppliers of East Lancs or Northern Counties. Number 576 was one of a batch of forty-six supplied by East Lancs in early 1974 and was photographed in Market Street on 29 May 1979. NCT operated a fleet of 377 Atlanteans alongside a number of Daimler Fleetlines.

J. Fishwick & Sons of Leyland operated a curious mix of fourteen Atlanteans, the first eight of which were lowbridge models. Number 18 was one of four with East Lancs bodies and was new in August 1974. It is now preserved and is seen at the Golden Hill garage on 12 July 2007 whilst taking part in a Fishwick centenary rally.

One of the most peculiar Atlanteans of all was possibly the one featured above on 10 July 1976. HHT 57N was purchased new by Hale-Trent Cakes of Clevedon in Somerset in March 1975 and was purely used as staff transport, along with a number of other buses. Note it has no destination screen. The factory closed in 1987, two years after merging with Lyons Bakery. (Andrew Harvey-Adams)

Borough of Preston's first East Lancs-bodied Atlanteans were obtained in September/November 1976. They were sold on in 1989/90, six to Sheffield Omnibus and four to Warrington Borough Transport. Number 113 (formerly Preston No. 117) is seen in Sankey Street in Warrington on 17 July 1996. The operator also had thirty-four similar-looking buses that were purchased new.

As previously mentioned, South Yorkshire PTE had an eclectic mix of body styles including two classic early-style East Lancs-bodied examples which were a cancelled order by Fishwick. Numbers 322/3 joined the PTE fleet in October 1976. The second of the duo is seen at Herries garage in 1985. (John Law)

As previously mentioned, Brighton Corporation had some classic East Lancs-style Atlanteans. Twenty dual-door buses joined the fleet in 1975/7 followed by a batch of fifteen single-door versions in 1978. Number 66 is seen at Old Steine on 8 June 1977 when only a few months old. Five more Atlanteans with Northern Counties bodywork were acquired from Nottingham City Transport in 1979.

Blackpool Transport clung onto their PD3 back-loaders well beyond most other operators and didn't invest in any 'OPO' double-deckers until 1977. Numbers 301–10 were the first of sixty-two more or less identical buses which entered the fleet from 1977 to 1983. Last of the initial batch, No. 310, is seen in St Anne's Road and has just passed under the closed Blackpool direct line (closed in 1965), which led into Blackpool Central station (closed 2 November 1964), on 6 August 1983. This bus was destroyed by fire on 1 October 1986.

Preston Borough received its second batch of ten East Lancs-bodied Atlanteans in 1977. These were again of the AN68A/2R type (33-foot G2 gearbox) dual-door eighty-two-seaters. Number 124 is seen in a long line of buses parked in St Thomas' Road having been part of a forty-eight-bus contingent to transport schoolchildren to nearby Moor Park in connection with a visit of HM Queen Elizabeth II.

One of Warrington Borough's own Atlanteans as opposed to a second-hand example, No. 76 was new in December 1977 and is seen crossing Bank Hall Bridge over the River Douglas at Tarleton on 20 August 1978 whilst taking part in the Ribble Enthusiast's Club road run from Blackpool to Southport.

In 1973 and 1978 Sheffield Transport/South Yorkshire PTE bought moderate-size batches of East Lancs-bodied Atlanteans; these were of the flat windscreen style. First of the latter was No. 1576, which is seen in Hall Gate in Doncaster town centre with commemorative lettering for '80 years of public transport in Doncaster'. (Richard Simons)

Looking somewhat similar in style to the South Yorkshire example is Blackburn Borough Transport No. 125. This bus was one of six received in June 1979 and is painted in the later predominantly cream livery. It was photographed in Accrington's Peel Street bus station on 10 October 1992 waiting to depart on the inter-town service to Darwen. Blackburn Atlantean No. 17 is parked behind.

Comparison between this Southampton Atlantean and the picture of No. 115 on p. 31 would show that the two buses are virtually identical, yet No. 236 featured above is eleven years its junior. Completing this picture recorded in Pound Tree Road on 25 July 1981 are similar buses Nos 211, 237 and 241.

Plymouth City Transport's East Lancs-bodied Atlanteans were a little more stylish than others, having a curve above the windscreen. Number 143 was new in December 1979 and is seen parked alongside Roe-bodied No. 134 in Bretonside bus station on 7 August 1985. It was one of just two buses out of an order for twelve that was single-door.

The Merseyside PTE initially bought Alexander-bodied Atlanteans, in amongst which was a batch of fifty with bodies by East Lancs in 1973. The Lancashire firm then received orders for eighty more buses in the late 1970s. However, No. 1831 was one of a following protracted order for twenty-two buses delivered between May 1979 and March 1980. It is seen with a quartet of Preston Borough Atlanteans, Nos 2 and 173–75, on Southport Promenade on 16 July 1983 in connection with the Open Golf Championships at Royal Birkdale.

Hyndburn Transport bought their last two new Atlanteans in August 1980. Number 199 is seen at Blackburn Boulevard working one of the Hyndburn circular routes on 10 November 1984. Hyndburn would later purchase a number of second-hand Atlanteans, most notably from Merseyside, Plymouth, Preston and Ribble.

Rossendale was another operator who bought new Atlanteans and then later supplemented them with second-hand purchases. In total Rossendale bought fourteen new Atlanteans including Nos 24, 21 and 19, which are depicted above on the M66 motorway on the occasion of Pope John Paul II's visit to Heaton Park in Manchester on 31 May 1982.

Ipswich Borough Transport also specified the flat windscreen for their final batch of four Atlanteans obtained in May 1981. These followed a solitary East Lancs-bodied example, which was delivered to the undertaking in the previous November. Roe bodywork had previously been specified. Number 40 was photographed in Crown Street on 13 September 1982. Note the elaborate fleet number style.

City of Lancaster (CoL) only bought their first Atlanteans in December 1979. The operator went on to purchase nineteen new buses of the type in total, all with East Lancs bodies. Number 204, which was new in 1981, is seen in Friargate in Preston on 11 February 1989 on the jointly (with Preston Borough) operated service 40 from Lancaster. CoL also added a significant number of second-hand Atlanteans to its fleet.

Plymouth City Transport's (Plymouth Citybus) last thirty-six Atlanteans were completed by East Lancs and were received in 1979–81. Numbers 162–71 were the last Atlanteans of all and were of chassis type AN68B/1R with single-door bodywork. Number 165 is depicted in Royal Parade in the city centre on 7 August 1985.

One of Nottingham's first East Lancs-bodied Atlanteans was featured on p. 34. Number 461 was one of the last batch provided by the Lancashire firm in February 1982. This scene was recorded in Long Row on 12 June 1984. Behind is similar bus No. 405, which has replaced the Northern Counties-bodied Atlantean of the same number featured on p. 68.

Blackpool Transport's sixth batch of Atlanteans comprised just four buses, which arrived in August 1982. These had the rounded corners at the front. Seen in a somewhat simplified version of the Blackpool livery, No. 354 was photographed in North Albert Street in Fleetwood on 9 August 1995. It still has a 'Pay on Entry' box on the front.

Looking fairly similar is Preston Bus No. 168. This was one of an order for seven buses that were received in November/December 1982. They were originally dual-door and painted in the mid-blue and ivory livery. The two-tone blue and cream livery was introduced in 1999. Photographed in Black Bull Lane on 15 October 2003.

Lancaster's last three Atlanteans were completed to a higher specification, which included the fitting of high-backed seats. These were Nos 221–3, which were new in 1983/4. Following the takeover by Stagecoach in 1993, CoL's new Atlanteans were retained by the new owner and No. (1)222 is seen departing Preston bus station on 15 November 1993 on service 167 to Blackpool.

Borough of Preston's last two Atlanteans were similarly upgraded with high-backed seats and the same dipped side front windows. Numbered 1 and 2, they were also painted differently and were delivered as single-door buses. Number 1 (later renumbered to 181 and re-seated) is seen shortly after delivery in the Deepdale Road garage Dock Shop on 18 June 1983. Preston's last Atlanteans were withdrawn from service on 20 July 2007.

Blackburn's last East Lancs-bodied Atlanteans were also of a similar appearance but were of a standard H43/31F layout. Having re-adopted this attractive layout of the olive green and cream livery, two-year-old No. 24 sparkles in the sun at the Boulevard on 11 May 1985. Ribble Leyland National No. 821 completes the picture in a world before bus deregulation.

Blackpool Transport (BTS) also followed suit by specifying high-back seats in their last two Atlanteans. Blackpool Nos 363/4 were the last Atlanteans to be bodied by East Lancs and were delivered to the operator in September 1984. Number 364 is seen on rail replacement duties at Preston station on 28 September 1985. It wasn't withdrawn by BTS as an active vehicle until 30 November 2009 and has been retained as a heritage bus.

ECW

Eastern Coach Works (ECW) were a moderate player in the Atlantean story, producing just 253 Atlanteans. Their main source of revenue was of course the Bristol fleets and particularly the VRT model. The first Atlanteans bodied by ECW were a small batch of four for Ipswich Corporation in October 1968. Number 73, along with Roe-bodied No. 15, is seen at the Tower Ramparts bus station on 26 May 1978. All four passed to Eastbourne Buses in 1980 with two being converted to open-top buses.

Leicester City Transport only operated twenty-three Atlanteans. These comprised three with Metro-Cammell bodies and ten each from Park Royal and ECW. Both the latter are represented in this picture of Nos 106 and 96 taken inside the Abbey Park Road garage on 3 March 1976. Note the pristine 'Atlantean' badges on the front of both buses.

ECW also constructed bodies on buses ordered by former BET fleets. Northern No. 3236 (originally Gateshead & District No. 112L) was a 1972 PDR1A/1 which, as can be seen, was of dual-door configuration. Gateshead & District used six different body builders to complete their eighty-eight Atlanteans. Seen at Gateshead Interchange on 26 June 1982.

Whilst Colchester Corporation's first Atlanteans had Massey-built bodies, when the operator returned to the improved chassis type for its requirements in 1975, all subsequent orders were bodied by ECW; all of the undertaking's Atlanteans were of a H43/31F layout. Numbers 61 and 65 were photographed outside the Town Hall in the High Street on 26 May 1978. The building was designed by John Belcher and constructed between 1897 and 1901. It is Grade I listed.

Ribble Motors was ECW's largest customer when it came to the Atlantean with eighty-two chassis of the type being completed by the Suffolk firm over a period of four years. As per the Colchester buses, these were again of H43/31F configuration. Number 1433 was new in 1976 and is seen in the village of Clifton whilst working from Preston to Blackpool on 2 April 1980.

The last two Atlanteans bodied by ECW were both one-off demonstrators for Leyland Vehicles, with both passing to J. Fishwick & Sons and then being saved for preservation. GRN 895W was a AN69/1R (0.690 engine) model that was new in February 1981. It is seen in its guise as Fishwick No. 23 on a Ribble Vehicle Preservation Trust (RVPT) running day at Lytham Hall on 26 August 2019.

The second ECW-bodied demonstrator didn't emerge as a completed bus until three years later and the chassis was originally designated as AN69/2L, indicating that it was left-hand drive. However, it was converted to right-hand drive before being sent to ECW to be bodied – the resultant bus resembled the Olympian style of body. Later assuming the role of Fishwick No. 2, it is seen at another RPVT event at Morecambe on 26 May 2019.

Fowler

For such a small operator Fishwick's collection of buses was anything but dull. This strange-looking four-year-old vehicle (bearing a resemblance to a character from the *Addams Family* 1960s TV programme) was No. 6 in the Fishwick fleet and was the only double-deck body to be constructed by the associated company of W. H. Fowler. It is seen alongside County Hall descending Fishergate Hill in Preston on Fishwick's flagship service (now operated by Stagecoach) sometime in 1976. Following withdrawal it passed to local Preston operator Mercer's Travel. (John Law)

Marshall

Equally rare in the Atlantean fold was this single-deck model, which had been bodied by Marshall of Cambridge. Great Yarmouth Corporation received three of the type in March 1968. Only Merseyside PTE (Birkenhead) and Portsmouth had any other new single-deck Atlanteans. Number 40 was saved for preservation and is seen in Cardiff on 26 June 1983 on the occasion of the city operator's centenary celebrations.

Other than the three buses for Great Yarmouth the only other Atlanteans bodied by Marshall were a batch of thirty for South Yorkshire PTE in 1981; these were also the operator's (and its predecessor's) last Atlanteans, having operated a grand total of 653 since 1959. Number 1808 was photographed on a Rotherham local service in Centenary Way sometime during the 1980s. (Richard Simons)

Massey

Massey's contribution to the Atlantean model was just thirty-one vehicles, which were built for three operators. Maidstone Borough received twenty Massey-bodied PDR1/1s between 1965 and 1968. A number were loaned to London Country in 1977 and No. 29 of the first batch was caught on camera at Croydon bus station on 8 June 1977.

Colchester Borough Transport had ten very similar-looking machines, one of which was later rebuilt as an open-top bus. Number 47 had been repainted into a simplified livery when it was photographed in Osborne Street on 26 May 1978. It was sold out of service in 1980.

Besides the buses for Colchester and Maidstone the only other Atlantean to be completed by Massey was this PDR1/1, which was obtained by A. Hunter of the A1 Buses consortium. KSD 661F is seen in Dalry Road (near the junction of Anderson Drive) in Saltcoats on 12 April 1978. All the Massey-bodied Atlanteans were to the same H43/31F configuration.

Metro-Cammell

Metro-Cammell was the second largest provider of bus bodies for the Atlantean chassis and indeed supplied the first of the type to enter public service. These comprised five lowbridge types for James of Ammanford and six highbridge models for Wallasey Corporation in December 1958. Wallasey No. 1 later passed to the Merseyside PTE as No. 201. It was withdrawn in 1977 and passed into preservation. It was photographed in Birkenhead taking part in a vintage running day on 2 October 2016.

Ribble operated three former Atlantean demonstrators that had been acquired with local Lancashire Independents Bamber Bridge Motor Services and Scout Motors. 398 JTB was new in 1959 and ran as No. S2 in the Scout fleet. It was acquired by Ribble in 1961 and given the number 1970. It is seen departing Preston bus station on 31 March 1973. Despite over two years having passed since the formation of the NBC the Ribble livery is still very much in evidence in this view. (Alan Snatt)

Sheffield City Transport's first Atlanteans were obtained in October 1959 and comprised Metro-Cammell-bodied Nos 363–8 and 881–99, a total of twenty-five buses. Number 884 was found resting in the Pond Street bus station parking ground on 31 March 1975.

Kingston-upon-Hull City Transport amassed a fleet of 241 Atlanteans, all of which had Roe bodywork, except the first five that had been bodied by Metro-Cammell. These passed to the West Midlands PTE and the former Hull No. 345 (WMPTE No. 1145) is seen in Dudley bus station on 19 May 1976.

Besides its unusual single-deck Atlanteans Great Yarmouth Corporation also had a small contingent of double-deck PDR1/1s. Metro-Cammell-bodied No. 4, dating from 1960, is seen with Roe-bodied No. 6, four years its junior, behind on the Regal bus stand in Dene Side on 5 June 1975. The Regal Theatre was demolished in 1989 and was replaced by the Market Gates Shopping Precinct.

The only Atlanteans originally built to an open-top format were nine examples for Devon General in May 1961 – and even these had removable roofs. They spent most of their normal existence on the south coast around Torquay and were affectionately known as 'Sea Dogs' owing to their seafaring names. Several later found other homes and at least five of the nonet were thought to be still in existence in 2023. Originally Devon General No. DL931 *Sir Thomas Howard*, this preserved example was photographed on Morecambe Promenade on a vintage RVPT bus running day on 22 May 2022.

Birmingham City Transport only ever operated eleven Atlanteans, one of which was a former demonstrator. Numbers 3231–40 were new in November 1961 and passed to the WMPTE in October 1969. Class leader No. 3231 is seen in heavy traffic in Digbeth in April 1974 as it heads north from Hall Green to Pheasey. Service 90 was still a crew-operated route at the time. Standard Daimler No. 3224 is in pursuit. (Andrew Harvey-Adams)

Plymouth City Transport converted three of its 1962 Metro-Cammell-bodied Atlanteans to open-top format in 1975/6. Number 158 (later renumbered to 458 and named *Plymouth Adventurer*) remained with the operator until 1991, after which it saw further service on the Yorkshire coast. It is seen taking part in a bus rally at Harrowiside in Blackpool on 24 June 2007.

As previously mentioned, Leicester City Transport bought three Atlanteans with Metro-Cammell bodies, Nos 185–87, in February 1963. They were sold by Leicester in 1979. The former No. 187 was photographed in the yard of Continental Pioneer at Richmond on 17 April 1982. The yard was adjacent to Richmond station (having previously been railway sidings) with access from Cedar Terrace – the site was sold for residential redevelopment in mid-1985.

Bury Corporation added fifteen Metro-Cammell-bodied PDR1/1s to its fleet in April 1963; these incorporated the peaked dome that featured on Liverpool's first Atlanteans in late 1962. Now part of the Greater Manchester fleet, No. 6315 (ex-Bury No. 115) was captured alongside the former Ramsbottom UDC bus garage on 9 March 1975.

Portsmouth's first fifty-four Atlanteans were bodied by Metro-Cammell and joined the fleet in four batches from 1963–6. The former No. 222 was new in 1963 and withdrawn in 1975. Six of the type were purchased by East Staffordshire District Council with No. 222 becoming No. 2 in the Midlands fleet. It was photographed on Burton Bridge on 24 September 1977. It was withdrawn the following year.

Salford City Transport bought two Atlanteans in 1962 with Metro-Cammell bodies followed by a further three in 1964 and batches of twenty-one in each of the years 1965 and 1968. The last twenty of a grand total of sixty-seven were new in 1969 with Park Royal bodies. One of the 1964 trio, No. 210 (by then Greater Manchester No. 3056), is seen turning from Hanging Ditch into Cateaton Street in front of the Corn Exchange on 27 April 1975.

Plymouth amassed a fleet of one hundred Metro-Cammell-bodied Atlanteans before switching to Park Royal in 1968. Painted in a lighter red is No. 204, which joined the fleet in January 1966. Seen in Royal Parade on 22 July 1981, it was withdrawn the following year.

The Liverpool Corporation Met-Cams were quite distinctive with their peaked domes and aluminium bumpers. There were 380 of these 1960s buses in the fleet, all of which passed to the PTE in December 1969. Number L606 was still in Corporation green when photographed in Derby Square on 19 March 1976 whilst No. L718 was sporting the PTE's Verona green and cream. The Square has since been pedestriansied. Visible above L718 is the Castle Moat House, which was originally built for the North & South Wales Bank in 1838–40.

Former Liverpool Corporation Atlantean No. L646 was working for Fylde Borough when it was photographed in Squires Gate Lane on the St Annes/Blackpool border on 11 July 1978. It still retained all of its original Liverpool features. Number 92 was one of six of the type (including one for spares) acquired by the operator in 1977 – it was withdrawn in 1982.

Portsmouth City Transport 1964 Metro-Cammell PDR1/1 No. 237 was photographed in Isambard Brunel Road on 12 June 1976 passing Marshall-bodied Leyland Panther Cub No. 153. Number 237 was withdrawn in 1980 whilst Nos 249–52 of the 1966 batch were converted to open-top buses in 1977–79.

Bolton Corporation bought a second batch of Metro-Cammell-bodied Atlanteans in 1965 consisting of just eight buses. The former No. 224 (GM Transport No. 6724) was parked up in Moor Lane bus station on 29 November 1975. Alongside is East Lancs-bodied example No. 250 (GMT No. 6750).

In 1978 CoL acquired twelve former Salford/GMT Atlanteans (inclusive of two for spares). Four of these were converted to open-top buses in 1980/1. Last of these to be done was No. 218 *Lady Diana* (the second of four names it carried), which is seen in Heysham Road in Morecambe on 21 June 1981.

Another operator to avail itself of MPTE's redundant Met-Cams was the Isle of Man National Transport; fourteen of the type were acquired in 1979. This trio, seen in the Douglas garage yard, comprises former MPTE Nos L736/50/2, then IOMNT Nos 80/2/8. Also visible is former Tyne & Wear Alexander-bodied PDR2/1 No. 677 (IOMNT No. 64).

For a number of years Manchester Corporation divided its PSV orders between Daimler and Leyland. A total of 142 standard front-entrance Metro-Cammell-bodied PDR1s were purchased in three batches from 1960–6. One of the last was No. 3851, which was receiving attention in Piccadilly bus station on 4 May 1976. Service 59 to Shaw via Oldham was a long-established route. The route as far as Oldham was part of the Bee Network in 2025.

A quiet scene amongst the splendour of Grosvenor Gardens in London's Victoria district sees former Portsmouth Metro-Cammell-bodied Atlantean No. 247 keeping company with Limebourne 1980 Roe-bodied Atlantean JWF 47W. The latter was the sole Atlantean purchased new by Limebourne whilst the former was now in the ownership of Maybury & Sons Coaches Ltd (later known as the Big Bus Company). Completing the picture on 1 May 1983 is LT Airbus Metrobus No. M440 on the A1 service to Heathrow Airport.

In 1966 Bournemouth purchased a batch of twenty Atlanteans with Metro-Cammell bodywork that looked very similar to Alexander's product. In 1976 Tyne & Wear experienced a chronic shortage of buses and Bournemouth No. 201 was one of several Provincial Atlanteans that came to the rescue. It was photographed in Blackett Street in Newcastle on 26 May with Tyne & Wear PTE Alexander-bodied Atlantean No. 238 behind.

Newcastle Corporation also bought some Metro-Cammell-bodied Atlanteans of their own. Again looking very much like an Alexander product, Tyne & Wear PTE No. 212 (originally Newcastle No. 112) was also photographed in Blackett Street on 26 May 1976. Newcastle Corporation/Tyne & Wear PTE purchased a total of 641 Atlanteans from 1960–80. The Universal Building Society functioned as such from 1863 to 2006.

BOAC bought fifteen Atlanteans in 1966 which were fitted with Metro-Cammell coach-seated bodies. They added a further five with Roe bodywork in 1971. Two of the Met-Cams, LYF 316/7D, are seen at the Victoria Air Terminal in Buckingham Palace Road on 21 March 1974. Alongside is Duple-bodied Bedford SB3 FMC 191B. The terminal was opened as The Imperial Airways Empire Terminal on 5 June 1939 and closed to passengers on 14 November 1980 – it is now part of the National Audit Office. (KDH Archive)

Leeds City Transport's first three batches of Atlanteans had bodywork by Weymann, Metro-Cammell and Park Royal, respectively, before Roe dominated the scene from 1970 onwards. The Met-Cams were a batch of fifteen buses that dated from December 1966. Number 352 was still in its original two-tone green when photographed in New Market Street in the city centre on 7 May 1976. The direction gantry has long since been removed.

Prior to Bradford Corporation buying dual-door Alexander-bodied Atlanteans, the operator bought two batches of PDR1s with single-door Metro-Cammell bodywork, each consisting of fifteen buses. Number 296 belonged to the second batch, which were new in October 1968. On 28 February 1982 it was parked outside Stonier's Tunstall garage in Parsonnage Street in Stoke-on-Trent.

After 1968 Metro-Cammell built just 165 bodies for the Atlantean chassis, with the principal customers being London Country, Maidstone & District, Merseyside PTE and the Tyne & Wear PTE. Those for London Country were just the second batch of Atlanteans received by the NBC operator in October 1972. Number AN120 is seen passing LT Routemaster No. RM140 in Bromley Common on 29 May 1982.

The very last Atlantean chassis bodied by Metro-Cammell (MCW) were a batch of thirty AN68A/1Rs for the Tyne & Wear PTE in August 1979. Number 231 was captured in Grainger Street in Newcastle city centre on 26 June 1982.

Neepsend

Neepsend was a subsidiary of East Lancs situated in Penistone Road in Sheffield. In total they only completed forty-nine bodies on Atlantean chassis. Sheffield City Transport took three batches of buses from 1964–6, which accounted for forty vehicles. Number 354, of 1965, is seen in the Pond Street bus park on 22 May 1976.

The remaining nine Atlantean bodies completed by Neepsend consisted of four buses for Bolton Transport and five for Oldham Corporation. These all had the look of their parent company, East Lancashire Coachbuilders. Greater Manchester Transport No. 5152 (originally Oldham Corporation No. 152) was new in April 1967 and was photographed at Oldham Mumps in June 1979. (John Cronshaw)

Northern Counties

Nottingham City Transport No. 405 was one of the first ten Atlantean chassis bodied by Northern Counties of Wigan, in November 1964. It was somewhat reminiscent of Fowler's Fishwick No. 6, although it predated it by eight years. It was recorded in Long Row West in Nottingham on 13 November 1975.

AA Motor Services and Yorkshire Traction were Northern Counties' next customers before Ribble took a batch of fifteen in June 1967. Other than Merseyside these buses moved all around Ribble's operating area, as demonstrated by this picture of No. 1961 in Carlisle's Lowther Street bus station on 8 August 1977. At the time it was one of three of the type based at Penrith garage.

The Northern Counties look did vary a bit depending on the individual customer's requirements. Teesside Transport bought fifteen of these dual-door squareish-looking Atlanteans in 1970 having previously purchased their buses from Roe and Park Royal. Number A51 was picking up passengers in the centre of Stockton-on-Tees on 30 May 1975.

Lytham St Annes Corporation (later Fylde Transport) styled their first Northern Counties-bodied Atlanteans on the Nottingham look. Numbers 75–7 joined the undertaking in November 1970 and gave good service until 1983 (Nos 75/6) and beyond (No. 77). Number 75 is seen in Squires Gate Lane on 5 July 1977. Fylde had four acquired former Hull Atlanteans rebuilt by Northern Counties as single-deck buses in 1993. They were originally numbered 4–7; No. 7 is now preserved.

A second operator to run single-deck Atlanteans was the Merseyside PTE in the form of Nos 95/6. These two dual-door buses had been ordered by Birkenhead Corporation but were delivered to the PTE in January 1971. Number 95 was resting inside Walton garage on 26 April 1981.

Graham's of Paisley didn't buy any new Atlanteans but assembled a small fleet of second-hand examples and Daimler Fleetlines. The garage was situated in Hawkhead Road, which is where former Maidstone Borough Northern Counties Atlantean No. 47 was residing with former Nottingham Fleetline No. 57 on 12 April 1978. The company ceased trading on 29 April 1990.

Wigan Corporation used to divide its body orders between the two local firms of Massey and Northern Counties. However, the latter absorbed the former before Wigan received its first Atlantean in November 1968. Wigan Corporation didn't join the Manchester PTE until 1 April 1974 and the undertaking's last ten Atlanteans in May 1972 were the first of the new improved AN68/1R chassis type to be bodied by any coach builder. GMT No. 3339 (originally Wigan No. 10) is seen in Market Street in Wigan on 21 April 1984.

Once Massey Brothers had been taken over by Northern Counties some customers transferred to the parent company. Maidstone Borough's last two batches of Atlanteans were completed by Northern Counties. Number 52 joined the fleet in June 1972 and was photographed in the town's High Street when just three years old. Behind is new Willowbrook-bodied Bedford YRQ No. 57.

Like AI the AA Motor Services group served the Ayrshire Coast around Ayr and Troon. The principal operator was Young of Ayr, who purchased seven of the eight new Atlanteans operated by AA. New in December 1972 on an AN68/1R chassis, YSD 309L is thought to be in Loans Main Street, although the houses in the background cannot be traced. The picture was recorded on 27 March 1976.

Delaine of Bourne near Peterborough bought just two new Atlanteans. The first was a PDR1/1 model with a Willowbrook body in February 1966, whilst the second was ACT 540L, as seen above, which was an AN68/2R model with a Northern Counties-built body new in May 1973. Having been withdrawn from service in 2000, it has proved to be a survivor and is now owned by the Delaine Heritage Trust. It is seen resplendent in Bourne's attractive livery at Showbus at Donington on 30 September 2018.

Another independent operator to avail itself of the Atlantean was OK Motor Services of Bishop Auckland. Again these were just small numbers with three in March 1973 and one the year after joining the fleet. The latter was GCR 103N, which was photographed in the OK garage on 26 June 1982. The operator was acquired by Go Ahead in March 1995.

Northern Counties' biggest customer was undoubtedly Greater Manchester Transport. In conjunction with the PTE they developed what was termed 'the standard Manchester body', which was used on Atlanteans, Daimler Fleetlines and Leyland Fleetlines (from 1978). Northern Counties also provided the bodies on the GMT Fodens and Olympians. Number 7529 was new to the PTE in December 1974 and was caught resting outside the Town Hall in Albert Square on 15 May 1982.

To speed up production the PTE also engaged Park Royal, who provided 160 bodies in 1977–9 but then reverted solely to Northern Counties. Number 8537 was new in August 1982 but looked similar to the one above, which was eight years older. Commencing with No. 7001, all 1,225 Atlanteans to the end of the run in April 1984 were of the H43/32F configuration.

Barrow Borough Transport was a very late recipient of the Atlantean having only taken single-deck types for a number of years. However, in 1983 the undertaking bought a batch of three and added a fourth the following year. Number 105 was new in February 1983 and is seen in Duke Street in Barrow-in-Furness town centre on 1 September 1984.

The very last normal-production Atlantean to enter service in the UK was Fylde Borough Transport's Northern Counties-bodied AN68D/1R No. 75 in October 1984. It is seen here at the Squires Gate Lane garage on 16 June 1985. Like some other Lancashire municipals' Atlantean buses it was fitted with high-back seats. Number 75 was withdrawn in May 2004 and is now preserved in Seagull Coaches Blue Bus livery, having also worn Blackpool green and cream at one time.

Park Royal

The first Atlanteans bodied by Park Royal were received by Stockton-on-Tees Corporation in March/December 1964. Then followed one bus for Sheffield Transport and a demonstrator before the builder embarked on an order for London Transport for thirty-seven PDR1/1s in November 1965, quickly followed by a further thirteen. Number XA48 entered service at Highgate garage in January 1966. It was transferred to London Country in November 1969 and subsequently sold to China Motor Bus in April 1973. It was looking somewhat forlorn when photographed in Causeway Bay scrapyard in Hong Kong on 24 October 1981.

Following a single Park Royal-bodied Atlantean in November 1964, Sheffield next turned to the builder in 1966 when fifty-eight PDR1/2s were added to the fleet. These were all single-door models, although dual-door Park Royals would later follow. The stylish bodywork was carried by No. 158, which is seen at the Pond Street bus park on 31 March 1975. Alongside is East Lancs-bodied No. 320, which was new in May 1973.

Stockton-on-Tees/Teesside bought four small batches of Park Royal-bodied Atlanteans between 1966 and 1968. Number H16, of the third batch and now painted in Cleveland Transit green, is seen in Stockton High Street on 20 May 1978. The cinema behind was opened as The Regal in April 1935; it reopened as the Odeon thirty-three years later. *Close Encounters of the Third Kind* was showing at the time the picture was recorded.

Ralph Bennett was the forward-thinking General Manager of Manchester City Transport in the late 1960s and was responsible for a body style that was known as the 'Mancunian'. A total of 293 of these bodies were built by Metro-Cammell, Park Royal and Roe and mounted on Daimler Fleetline chassis. A further 199 were produced by East Lancs, Metro-Cammell and Park Royal for the Atlantean PDR1A/1 and PDR2/1 chassis. The last of the type were received in the SELNEC era. First off the Park Royal production line was No. 1001 in March 1968. It was withdrawn from service in the early 1980s and is now preserved. This view was taken outside the Greater Manchester Museum of Transport on 5 April 2009.

As previously noted, Leicester City Transport bought a batch of ten Park Royal-bodied Atlanteans in April 1969. On 10 September 1982 No. 112 was waiting to depart Humberstone Gate on service 61 to Nether Hall.

Greater Manchester Transport No. 3155 was new to Salford City Transport as No. 309 in July 1969. As can be seen, the style is very similar to the Leicester bus featured above. It was working off Wigan garage when photographed in Station Road in Wigan on 29 August 1981 with a service for Hindley Castle Hill. This area of Wigan was later substantially redeveloped.

Still a Park Royal vehicle but in a somewhat different style with a peaked dome. Plymouth City Transport purchased forty-three Atlanteans of this style from 1968–70. Two further batches bodied by Park Royal in 1971/5 were of the revised style, as illustrated on p. 81. Number 256 is seen in a short-lived revised livery in Royal Parade on 22 July 1981. The expansive Royal Parade was laid out in the late 1940s following extensive wartime bomb damage. The Debenhams store closed in 2021.

This Park Royal revised style became quite popular amongst operators particularly with London Country, Ribble and Southdown. Gateshead & District No. 209N (later Northern No. 3283) was new in August 1974 and was photographed at the Gateshead Metro Centre on 26 June 1982. The Interchange opened in November 1981; it was rebuilt in the early 2000s and reopened in March 2004.

As said, a number of NBC bus operators availed themselves of the Park Royal body style. Ribble Motors of Preston bought 104 such buses in 1974/5 before changing to ECW. They were mainly to be seen on Merseyside and in Central Lancashire, although a trio was based at Ambleside for service on the prestigious 555 route. Number 1363 is seen in Fylde Road in Preston on 29 June 1981 returning from Blackpool on the 158.

By comparison East Yorkshire bought fifteen of the type and Yorkshire Woollen eleven. The latter's No. 773 was having a day out in Blackpool when photographed in the coach park on 19 August 1979. In later life, whilst in private ownership, it operated on hire to Black Prince of Morley, an operator who had a varied collection of second-hand Atlanteans.

As referred to earlier, Plymouth Citybus also operated a number of Park Royal-bodied Atlanteans in the later style. Numbers 1–15 were new in March 1971 whilst Nos 76–90 followed in April 1975, after the undertaking stocked its fleet with a considerable number of Leyland Nationals. Number 88 is seen at Bretonside on 7 August 1985. The bus station was closed in 2016 and demolished the following year for redevelopment.

Greater Manchester's three main bus types of the 1970s/80s are captured in the same picture. On the left is Park Royal-bodied Atlantean No. 7844 whilst centre is Leyland Fleetline No. 8040 and on the right Daimler Fleetline No. 7418; the latter two have Northern Counties bodies, although the Park Royal bus is in a similar style to the others. Park Royal provided 160 bodies for GMT buses before the works closed in 1980. Piccadilly, 3 April 1982.

London Country's first ninety Atlanteans were bodied by Park Royal. These were followed by four further batches totalling sixty-three buses from 1974–80. Number AN127 was waiting to depart Kingston's Wood Street bus station on 17 April 1982. Alongside is LT DMS Fleetline No. 31 working off Sutton garage. Route 213A was later absorbed by the 213.

Roe

Roe's early bus bodies were somewhat boxy in appearance. They first produced a batch of twenty-three for Trent in March 1960. Three of their first five customers were based in the North East, as illustrated on Northern (originally Gateshead & District) No. 91 and seen in Grainger Street in Newcastle on 28 May 1976. The Newcastle Permanent Building Society is now a Savers convenience store.

Still with the boxy look were the early batches of Atlanteans received by Kingston-upon-Hull. Apart from the undertaking's first five buses the remainder of Hull's 241 Atlanteans were all bodied by Roe. Number 158, which was new in December 1961 as No. 358, was photographed outside Lombard Street garage on 12 July 1975. The garage was built in 1936 but was badly damaged in a bombing raid in May 1941. It was eventually rebuilt in 1952 but then closed again and a shopping complex was opened on the site in 2007.

Lincoln City Transport bought a total of just eight Atlanteans all with Roe bodywork. Number 96 (renumbered from 48) was one of a quartet bought in July 1964 and is seen turning from St Mary's Street into High Street on 21 May 1976. Four more followed in 1965 before the operator changed to Bristol VRTs.

Oldham Corporation operated a fleet of seventy-three Atlanteans that, other than the two small batches of East Lancs- and Neepsend-bodied buses, were all bodied by Roe. However, as can be seen above on No. 163 of 1967, they had a distinctive peaked dome. Additionally the last twenty were dual-door buses. Now preserved, it is seen at a bus rally in Heaton Park, Manchester, on 4 September 2016 in its original colours.

Following bus deregulation in 1986, Fylde Borough sought to increase its fleet and turned to Hull for a supply of redundant Atlanteans. They were painted very similar to the Fylde buses and didn't initially receive a repaint until later in their operating lives. Fylde No. 76 (ex-Hull No. 271) was one of twenty-six former Hull Atlanteans that operated for the undertaking. It was captured in St Annes Road West on 25 July 1987.

Roe also produced a version with panoramic windows, which was much favoured by Leeds City Transport. Number 465 was new to Leeds in March 1971. Now wearing the West Yorkshire PTE colours, it is seen approaching St Peter's Street in the city centre on 3 October 1984. Roe produced 571 bodies over an eleven-year period for the operator.

Very much in the style of the Leeds buses was this solitary 1973 Atlantean for A1 Motor Services. Docherty's OCS 345L is travelling from Ardrossan to Kilmarnock via Saltcoats, Stevenston, Kilwinning, Irvine and Dreghorn. This view was recorded in Byres Road in Kilwinning on 1 June 1976. There were three other new Roe-bodied Atlanteans in the A1 fleet.

There were a number of small independent operators in the Doncaster area, one of which was Thomas Severn of Dunscroft. Severn bought ten new Atlanteans from 1965–77 with all but one having Roe bodies. HUG 33N was one of two purchased in February 1975 and is seen at a temporary bus stop in Christchurch Street in Doncaster when virtually brand new. The operator was absorbed by the South Yorkshire PTE in March 1979. (Richard Simons)

Ipswich Borough Transport's vehicle intake in 1976 comprised ten dual-door Atlanteans with Roe bodywork. Numbers 11 and 14 were captured at the Tower Ramparts bus station on 26 May 1978. The last Ipswich Atlanteans to run in service were Nos 32–4 on 30 September 2000. Other than the provision of new bus shelters, the bus station looks much the same today.

A wet day in Plymouth as Roe-bodied Atlantean No. 100, in a special livery advertising sightseeing tours, was photographed passing East Lancs-bodied No. 138 in Saltash Road outside Plymouth (formerly North Road) station on 22 July 1981. Plymouth's last Atlantean in service was No. 171, which was kept in use until 15 October 2006.

Hornsby of Ashby purchased a single new Atlantean in January 1978. XFW 983S was an AN68/1R model with a seventy-six-seat front-entrance Roe body. On 31 May 1982 it had brought a full complement of pilgrims to Heaton Park in Manchester to hear Mass said by Pope John Paul II.

Nottingham City Transport's last batch of Atlanteans was a batch of ten with Roe bodies in February 1981. Strangely these were the only Roe-bodied Atlanteans purchased by NCT and the first with single doors since 1967. Number 467 is seen in Smithy Row/Long Row on 12 June 1984. NCT's last Atlanteans ran from Bulwell garage on 27 November 1999. The last Roe-bodied Atlanteans were built for Kingston-upon-Hull in January 1982.

Seddon

The only Atlanteans bodied by Seddon were twelve single-deckers for Portsmouth City Transport in June 1971. These had forty-seat dual-door bodywork on a Leyland PDR2/1 chassis. Number 194 was being used by the city council as a promotional vehicle and is seen on Preston Market Square on 20 January 1980. When new they were equipped to pull a luggage trailer and used on a service between The Hard and the Sealink Ferry terminals.

Van Hool

South Yorkshire PTE No. 431 was a one-off. The PTE bought a considerable number of Volvo Ailsas with the bodies built by Van Hool McArdle in Ireland. In February 1977 a single AN68A/1R chassis received a dual-door Van Hool body and was photographed in Sheffield's Pond Street bus station when relatively new. (Richard Simons)

Weymann

From January 1959 until March 1962 Weymann only built lowbridge bodywork on the Atlantean chassis other than for Ribble/Standerwick and Silver Star. The first Atlanteans completed were for Maidstone & District. Walsall Corporation took a single example in September 1959 numbered 841. Seen in West Midlands PTE colours as No. 841L, it was photographed in Carrs Lane in Birmingham in August 1976 heading for Boney Hay (Walsall, 1955).

Chesterfield Corporation added a batch of four lowbridge Weymann-bodied Atlanteans to its fleet in March 1960. Number 103 is seen inside the small but quaint Vicar Lane bus station on 3 March 1976. The bus station was closed in the mid-1980s and demolished in 1987.

East Midlands, Potteries (PMT), Ribble and Trent were all repeat customers for the lowbridge Atlantean. Those for Ribble were built by the parent company Metro-Cammell whilst PMT took four separate batches between August 1959 and October 1962. Number (L)823 of the second batch is seen in Church Street in Stoke-on-Trent on 29 March 1975. The shop behind the bus is now a newsagents.

Weymann worked with Ribble to produce the luxury coach the 'Gay Hostess', which was specially designed for long-distance motorway work. Number 1251 was the prototype that emerged in November 1959. This was followed by Nos 1252–65 in June 1960 and then Standerwick Nos 16–25 in August 1960 and finally Nos 26–37 in June 1961, a total of thirty-seven vehicles. Standerwick No. 29 is seen arriving at Victoria Coach Station in April 1966 with a service from the North West. (KDH Archive)

Ribble/Standerwick's 'Gay Hostess' buses were replaced on the London services in 1970/1 by Bristol VRLs. A dozen of the type passed to Tees-side Railless Traction in the North East and were based at Stockton-on-Tees. Number A65 was the former Standerwick No. 16 and was photographed in Stockton High Street on 30 May 1975 – how the mighty had fallen. The shopping centre has been refurbished and the steps done away with.

Other than the aforementioned, the first highbridge bodies produced by Weymann were for Newcastle Corporation in March 1962. Numbers 227–38 were seventy-eight-seat front-entrance buses mounted on a PDR1/1 chassis. Number 237 is seen in the guise of Tyne & Wear PTE No. 437 in Neville Street outside Newcastle Central station on 26 May 1976.

Sheffield City Transport bought three small batches of Weymanns in 1962, with each batch for use with a different subsidiary. Number 221 had originally been No. 1351 in the Sheffield JOC fleet. It was recorded in Commercial Street in Sheffield city centre on 30 April 1977. This section of road is now occupied by the Sheffield Supertram.

Ribble acquired two former lowbridge Weymann-bodied demonstrators. 661 KTJ was new in September 1959 whilst 2295 TE emerged in January 1963. Both ended up with Bamber Bridge Motor Services before becoming Ribble Nos 1966/7 in April 1967. The latter is seen arriving at Preston bus station on 13 September 1977 on one of the local jointly operated services.

Following an initial batch of lowbridge Atlanteans Maidstone & District bought several batches of highbridge buses. Numbers DH586–632 were completed by Weymann in 1963. Number 5621 (originally No. DH621) is seen in Cornwallis Terrace outside Hastings railway station on 3 June 1975. It was around a 30-mile journey to Maidstone. In 2023 service 12 started at Tenterden and ran to Maidstone.

Leeds City Transport's first Atlanteans were a batch of ten completed by Weymann in July 1965. Sporting West Yorkshire PTE colours, No. 334 was pictured in Leeds bus station on 7 May 1976. LCT/WYPTE went on to operate 626 new Atlanteans.

One of the earliest and one of the last lowbridge Atlanteans to be bodied by Weymann are seen on Preston North End's car park on 18 March 1978. City of Lancaster No. 768 was originally Trent No. 1368 and had been new in August 1959, whilst Fishwick No. 23 was new in February 1964. Fishwick bought another three of the type in June 1966, which proved to be the last Atlanteans provided by Weymann (completed at Metro-Cammell) before production was brought to an end in January 1966.

Willowbrook

The last significant body builder in the Atlantean story is Willowbrook of Loughborough, who completed a total of 119 buses. Somewhat against the local political regime was the order for twenty-two Atlanteans for Coventry Corporation. Carrying its West Midlands PTE number of 353Y, this example is seen at Harnall Lane garage. (Richard Simons)

Following the Coventry examples, single buses were provided for Whippet and Delaine before Devon General took a batch of six in May 1966. Sporting a similar grille to its predecessors, No. 528 was photographed in Triangle Place at Teignmouth in the early 1970s on a service bound for Torquay. (Martyn Hearson)

Brighton Corporation bought three batches of Atlanteans with dual-door Willowbrook bodies from 1971–3. Number 86 of the first batch was photographed at Old Steine on 8 June 1977. The Corporation then changed to East Lancs for subsequent Atlantean deliveries.

The story of Fylde Borough's Nos 78–83 is not straightforward. These six buses were ordered from W. S. Yeates at Loughborough but Yeates had no capacity to build them and sub-contracted the work to Willowbrook. The latter were overstretched at the time with an order for Nottingham and the buses ended up being built by Northern Counties to their standard design. Number 78 was captured in St Annes Road West on 22 June 1977.

Amongst the many batches of Atlanteans ordered by Liverpool Corporation/Merseyside PTE were two batches with Willowbrook bodies in 1980/1. A small number of these were acquired by Hyndburn Transport. The former PTE No. 1843 (Hyndburn No. 140) is seen alongside former Plymouth Roe-bodied No. 91 at the garage on 27 October 1990.

One of the strangest Atlanteans was D850 AVV, which was owned by Whippet of Fenstanton. It was an AN68/2L model that was originally part of a large order constructed by Willowbrook in 1980 for service in Baghdad. However, it never departed the UK and was later rebuilt to right-hand drive and acquired by Whippet in 1987. It is seen at the garage off Cambridge Road. The premises were sold to Stagecoach in 2009 whilst Whippet moved to Swavesey. (Malcolm Audsley)